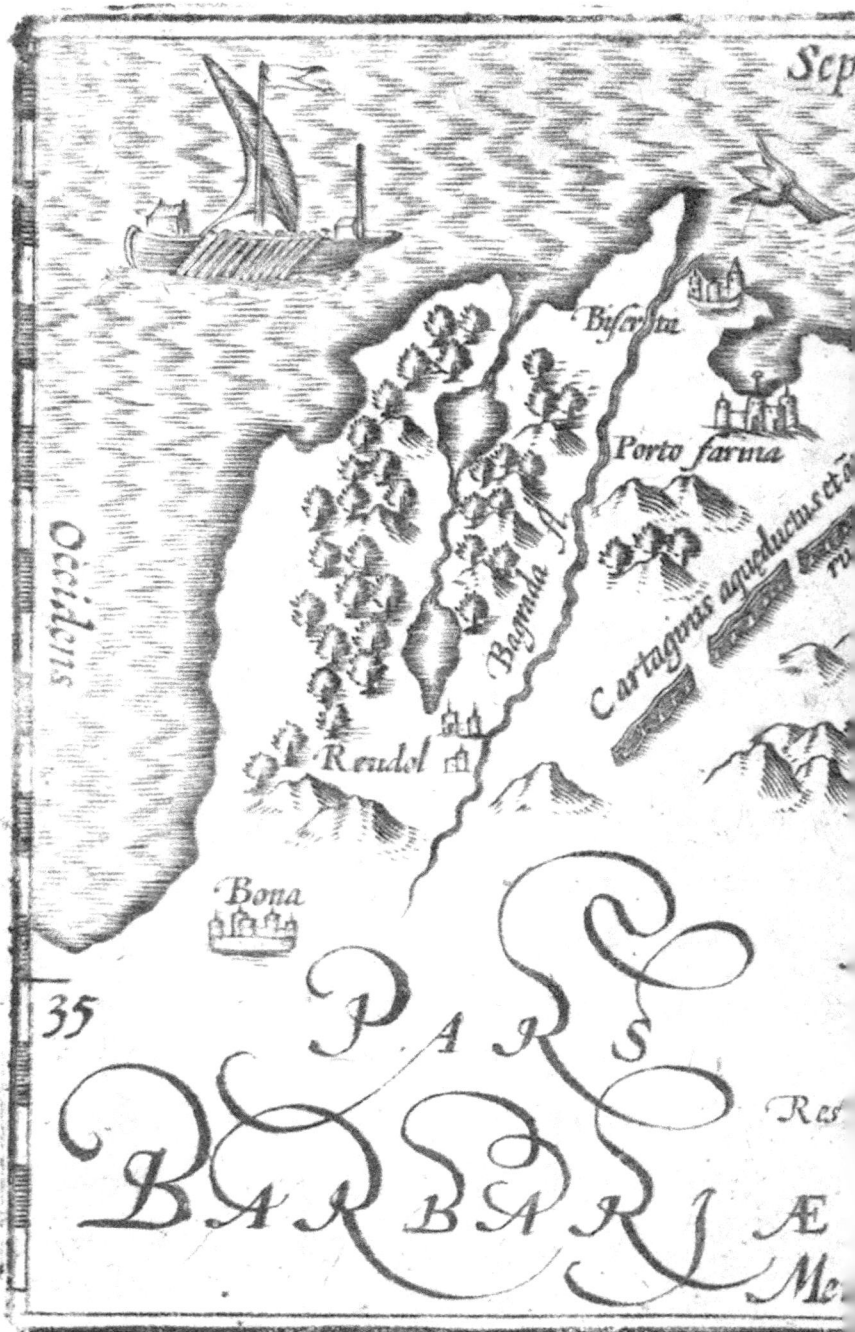

Sep

Occidens

Biferita

Porto farina

Bagrada fl.

Cartagnis aqueductus et ru

Reudol

Bona

35

PARS

Res

BARBARIÆ

Me

Zemol

C. Zaffran

C Bono olim
Prom Mercurij

Cupla

Pantalarea

Adrumen to

Ruspina

Carthaginensis

Thermarium ruina

Corada fl.

Goletta

Raba

Curza

Aphrica
ol Aphrodscum

Sinus

Cuzia

Tunus

Barde

Mecia

Carthaginen sis sinus

THE DESERT AT DUSK

THE DESERT
AT DUSK

Tahar Bekri

Translated by Peter Thompson

Contra Mundum Press   New York · London · Melbourne

The Desert at Dusk
© 2025 Peter Thompson;
Désert au crépuscule © 2018
Tahar Bekri (Al Manar éditions)

First Contra Mundum Press
edition 2025.

Library of Congress
Cataloguing-in-Publication
Data

    Bekri, Tahar
    The Desert at Dusk /
    Tahar Bekri

  —1st Contra Mundum Press
    Edition

132 pp., 5 × 8 in.

ISBN 9781940625782

   I. Bekri, Tahar.
  II. Title.
 III. Peter Thompson.
 IV. Translator.

2025936132

TRANSLATOR'S NOTE

Tahar Bekri has lived for almost fifty years in France. This introduces an obvious dualism in his work, and particularly in this apostrophe to the desert. There is the split consciousness (including, of course, emotional and poetic correlatives) that fellow Tunisian Amina Saïd has commented upon:

> The theme of wandering is very present in Maghrebi literature. It is at the same time choice & destiny, departures and returns, all of which create the desire for "place." Hence the image of the writer as forced like a tightrope walker to advance above an abyss. The source, also, of the impression of betweenness — possibly a privileged situation for a writer.[1]

There is also the gulf between the French and Arabic languages, and, for a modern writer (who also writes in Arabic) the split between modern and ancient registers of the latter. In this poetry we will see both pre-Islamic and Islamic themes,

---

1. *Marcher sur la terre* (Editions de La Différence) & *Walking the Earth* (Contra Mundum Press, 2024).

along with the duality of traditional praises of the desert next to its contemporary associations. And, less unique to Bekri, there is the "betweenness" of the poetic image — that is, the epistemological suspension between the two poles of comparison in metaphor or phanopoetic image. An example (a discussion of imagery follows): ... "the prayers recited backwards/like particles of soot." And then there is the dissonance between two central themes in this book: the poet's disgust with fanatic Islamist violence, and his idyllic childhood in the maritime palm grove.

Bekri's poetic desert has a ready reception among Maghrebi readers, including writers who write in French. In age he is between the two who follow. The first, the distinguished 82-year old Abdellatif Laâbi, is also an exile in France:

[...]
Voilà son massage
ambigu et sans appel
Imprévisible désert!

Il berce la créature
pour la détacher de l'attente
et lui faire miroiter la venue

Il laisse les tombes ouvertes
pour la routine de la résurrection

A sa manière
il improvise

En cela
il reste juvénile

Sa première page se remplit à peine
d'une écriture assez illisible

Et le sable qui s'en mêle
avec sa manie de la propreté
Le silence qui ne desserre pas son étau
ferme la marche
à double tour
pour que le désert retourne à lui-même
retrouve son hésitation
la somnolence de sa couleuvre
et la fraîcheur de sa malice

(excerpt, *Fragments d'une genèse oubliée*, 1997)

And, a full generation younger, fellow Moroccan Rachid Khaless:

Car
suffirait-il aux hommes de dérouler
                              [longuement leurs yeux
sur le désert
luisant et versatile
suppliant
invoquant pour que leur soit fait don de l'acte?
Leurs doigts seront greffés au sable
                              [et leurs fronts
obstruant la transe du vent, car
qui seront-ils dans le désert?
Hommes sans signes sans patronymes; hommes
de toutes saisons que tes siroccos
modèleront.

(from *Cantique du désert*, 1996)

These poems fully share — with Bekri — the cultural embrace of the *turath*, the social and artistic legacy that enriches the work of Maghrebi writers & intellectuals. Bekri's poems in *The Desert at Dusk*

have a more block-like form, more likely to physi-
cally suggest the *mu'allaqât* of Arabic lore — poems
which were suspended on the Black Stone in
Mecca. In his preface to this translation, he is ex-
plicit about this evocation. We will see that, while
the two writers above & many others have deftly
woven new images into the tradition of odes to
the desert, Bekri's appeal to pre-Islamic forms has
an especially lively confrontation with one of his
contemporary themes.

This thread (nostalgia) is at the heart of books
like *Le livre du souvenir*,[2] though the book is a tale
of wandering and diverse humanity. Similarly, *Je
Te Nomme Tunisie*[3] implies a deep nostalgia for the
country while decrying the catalysts of the Arab
Spring. Poem XIV, "Oh Selma," works a different
kind of feeling for the past; it is to some extent a
counterpoint & imitation of ancient Arab poetry
(see the note for this poem — and is closely related
to Bekri's book of "Selma" poems: *Poèmes à Selma*
(written in Arabic).[4] We note that, while a long
suite of these nostalgia poems occurs near the end
of *The Desert at Dusk*, there the book runs cruelly
into its other main theme.

2. Editions Elyzad, 2007.
3. Editions Al Manar, 2011.
4. Editions L'Harmattan, 1996.

Recognize poem XLI for what it is, a list of the sites of Islamic fundamentalist (*jihadi*, in a perversion of the concept of *jihad*) attacks on the public. Wahhabi, Isis (Daesh), and Al-Qaeda are the new monsters in Bekri's desert. Note that most of his references to them are bound up with desert terminology — as if (and it's not much of an exaggeration) this is their provenance. Bekri's bulwark against them is, first, the indignation of most Muslims and non-Muslims,[5] added to the posture of international criminal law. In a logical yet striking way this first reaction echoes an entire book by Moroccan poet & novelist Mohamed Hmoudane. Many of those poems are remarkably similar, in both form and content, to Bekri's:

> May every sword brandished
> And speaking for my dreams
> Drink unto drunkenness
> To feed the great blaze
> Split the sky
> Pulverize the stars
> In infinite metaphors
> Sketched on desert sand

5. See, from the Muslim world, Amin Maalouf's *Identités meurtrières*.

In nomad letters
Snaking one by one
From dune to dune
In the wake of caravans
And slave-raids far
From Yemen to the Levant
Antioch to Chang'an …

Hmoudane's target is made clear many times, as here: "And the fighter in the new fantasy caliphate/ Lumpen-terrorist with video games for a baby bottle."[6]

Hmoudane, like Bekri, invokes the purity of a distant past in references to Scheherazade, Abyssinia, the pre-Islamic era. But here one similarity ends. The second thrust of Bekri's reaction to unholy *jihad* has the emotional weight of something personal. It is as if part of his indignation derives from the desecration of something intimate — a contamination of his positive, nostalgic construction of the desert. His work is more animated and visceral than a consensus construct (traditional, Arab) of the dunes. Yet it is powerful as an assemblage — the candid and vulnerable juxtaposition of his beloved memories with their defilement.

6. Both citations from *Emergency!*, tr. of *Cas d'urgence* (Diálogos Books, 2020).

The above translations are mine. There are end-notes that will be helpful to most readers. At times they continue the above discussion about difficult images.

I should note the one significant formal change we have made. Bekri, like many Maghrebi poets — among them Rachid Khaless, Aicha Bassry, Hmou-dane, Ahmed Barakat and Saïd Kobrite (the latter two in their translations from Arabic) — adopts the convention of capitalizing the first letter of each line. As a convention, it is neutral, & usually absorbs itself without salient effect. But because this convention has largely been dropped in the Anglophone world its use can be somewhat dis-tracting. It is arguable that the convention gives some sense of the formality of ancient Arabic — an important source of texts for Bekri & perhaps a sentimental touchstone as well. My own opinion is that this "sense" withers when you consider that Arabic does not have capital letters, and if it did (and followed a similar convention) the capi-tal would be at the other (right hand) end of the line in any case. The approach taken in the present translation has the further advantage of occasion-ally disentangling syntax, by reserving upper case letters (at new lines) for new thoughts or images.

PETER THOMPSON

TEARS ON THE CHEEK
OF THE DESERT

I was born in a maritime palm grove in southern Tunisia. A miraculous garden that nourished my childhood and my imagination. It lies at the gateway to the desert. The latter, despite its aridity & harsh nature, has paradoxically carried a long and rich literary history, dating back to the pre-Muslim period, in 6th-century Arabia. Poetry predominates, an art conveyed by long poems, *qacidas,* called *mu'allaqâts* — poems that were hung on the walls of the Kaaba in Mecca after poetic contests between tribes. According to chroniclers of the time this took place in pagan Arabia, in Souk Ukâdh. The *mu'allaqâts* number seven or ten, depending on the version of literary history. Famous to this day, they constitute an important poetic heritage: a linguistic, cultural, ethnographic reference, a true source for the knowledge of Arab life before Islamization. Major themes of the *mu'allaqâts* include: life in the desert and what it requires in terms of prowess and valor, defense of the tribe and wars, epic life and endurance, love and chivalrous values, transhumance & nomadism, song and celebration of the natural and animal environment.

In middle and high school, I studied and memorized the *mu'allaqâts* that had an impact on me. They are part of my anchoring in the *turath*, my ancestral literary & cultural heritage. This distant poetic past is still present and vibrant within me, and I cannot conceive of the challenge of literary modernity to which I aspire without this demanding dialogue with the *turath*. For me, when the theme demands it, it is a rewriting, a rereading of History, where allegory, metaphor, allusion, and imagery are very present. Reality and imagination intertwine and interrogate me in an intertextual necessity.

My History is a terrain where I am torn in a constant back-and-forth in time & space, shaken by a conflicting ontological duality. Where ancient Arabia cannot be separated from the present Arab world, where current reality, although imbued with a glorious past, has tragic overtones.

The desert remains at the center of this antagonistic, contradictory vision, a land of fascination, beauty, and love songs, and at the same time, a place of distorting mirrors, turbulence, conflicts, wars, threats, failures, silting over, and defeats.

For half a century, to put it briefly, the Arab & Muslim world has experienced the rise of religious extremism presenting itself as a resurgence against the injustice of the era, as a solution to all ills. There is no need to say how dangerous & deadly this is, where faith is diverted for political ends, and aimed at seizing power.

I am a poet and citizen of the world, and I refuse to allow humanity to be sacrificed in the name of religion, justifying all kinds of unacceptable violence. I have only my pen to express the beauty of the world and my respect for humanity, on the side of life and peace, against the will for death. The poem cannot harbor those who hate mankind. Wherever they are, wherever they come from.

That is how the writing of this collection came to me, a speech that unites the happy memories of childhood, the desert sung in the poetry I learned, and the cruel & sinister current reality.

It was only natural for me to think about the form and structure of the *mu'allaqât*, and to write a book-poem, a long poem composed of short, autonomous poems, united by their theme, which connect evocations of ancient Arabia with the feelings aroused by current tragedy.

I experience the reality of the Arab & Muslim world in a dramatic way, even though I have lived in France for decades! Poetry cannot bury its head in the sand; it constitutes my moral conscience — my ethical duty, my duty toward beauty, in defense of the world.

The desert at dusk is the desert that lies in perdition, despite a pretense of wealth and artificial pomp. In the collection, it gradually becomes a metaphor for what we experience as terror, threat, violence, the sword of Damocles hanging over our heads!

I don't write out of simplistic, blissful, or exotic fascination, but out of the gravity of the world. I write against the sword & would like to oppose it with the pen of hope, of respect for humanity. I raise up the love poem, against hatred.

TAHAR BEKRI

"Behold this straw, even it
thinks always about truth"

Machrab

Uzbek poet, 17th–18th centuries

THE DESERT
AT DUSK

I

Ce n'est pas un mirage
Que tu vois au loin
Mais la caravane de chars
Les canons devant
Leurs outres assoiffées de sang
Cette eau asséchée
Comme gale sur la peau du goudron
Tant de sabres aux lames aiguisées
Aveuglent la poussière
Les bannières sourdes et noires

I

That's not a mirage
you see in the distance
but the caravan of tanks
Their gun barrels leading
and wineskins thirsting for blood
This water drying
like mange on the skin of the asphalt
So many swords their blades all sharpened
and blinding the dust
Their banners deaf and black

II

Et je t'entends gémir
Vieux désert
Que de palanquins d'opprobre
Portes-tu sur le dos
Des navires ensablés
Leurs bosses comme des fosses
Dans la fureur du firmament
Tous ces chameaux écumeux
Chancelants au seuil des demeures
Ne suffisent pour retenir les collines
Sous la rosée éplorée

II

And I hear you moan
Old Desert
How many palanquins of infamy
must you bear on your back
How many ships silted over
their humps like graves
in the rage of the firmament
All these foaming camels
staggering at the threshold of domains
can never hold back the hills
under this tearful dew

III

Dis vieux désert
Combien te faut-il de palmeraies orphelines
Pour consoler les palmes
Les ruines de ruines en ruines
Perdant le sommeil
La Nuit te fait-elle si peur
Cette voie lactée
Confondue avec la traînée de poudre
Les météorites fumantes
Dans les vallées de ton cœur

III

Tell me Old Desert
how many orphaned palm groves
will you need
to console the palms
The ruins of ruins lying in ruin
Is Night so frightening
while you sleep
This milky way
confused with the trail of dust
The smoking meteorites
in the valleys of your heart

IV

Et je te vois
Vieux désert
Réveillé en sursaut
D'éclat en éclat
Par les prières récitées à l'envers
Comme des fragments de suie
Les versets des fossoyeurs
Psalmodiés dans l'insolence des chenilles
Enterrant mes limons

IV

And I see you
Old Desert
startled awake
flash after flash
By the prayers recited backwards
like particles of soot
The verses of the gravediggers
chanted as the insolence of tank-tracks
buries my siltings

V

Dis vieux désert
Supportes-tu encore tous ces épouvantails
Dressés sur les chaires
Index et barbes sans gloires
Sermons et vindictes sans nombre
Tissant de toiles en grottes
Leurs bures d'ombre
Araignées promettant aux anges
Le paradis au bout de l'enfer

V

Tell me Old Desert
You still put up with these scarecrows
  propped on their pulpits
Index finger and beard yet glory wanting
Sermons and numberless condemnations
Spinning webs in caves
  for shadow vestments
Spiders who promise angels
a paradise at hell's end

VI

Dis
Vieux désert
Aux cheveux blanchis avant l'heure
Comment chasser tous ces chacals
Les crocs tout dehors
Leurs aboiements en rafales
Assourdissant plateaux et plaines
Déchirant les tentes portées
Sur les flancs des errances
Qui évitera aux vents tous ces pleurs

VI

Say
venerable Desert
your hair going white too soon
how to get rid of these jackals
their fangs always out
the gales of their baying
deafening plain and plateau
Ripping the tents laid against
the flanks of wandering
Who will spare the winds all this weeping

VII

Comment retenir la langue
Venimeuse des reptiles qui se meuvent
Sous terre
Les tunnels comme des terriers
Greniers pour les graines stériles
Rien ne pousse
Rien ne germe
Mais le rêve incendiaire
Ennemi de l'humanité entière

VII

How to restrain the venomous
tongue of the reptiles shifting
underground
Tunnels like burrows
Granges for sterile seeds
Nothing grows
Nothing sprouts
but the incendiary dream
enemy of all mankind

VIII

O vous campements
Abandonnés aux feux du crépuscule
Qui enchaîne mon insomnie
Les traces des étriers qui se cabrent
S'effacent dans les colonnes de fumée
Et vous amas de pierres
Las de soutenir les sépultures
Dois-je vous implorer
Pour panser mes fêlures
Les semelles en lambeaux
Sur les routes des convulsions

VIII

Oh you encampments
abandoned to the flames of a twilight
that enslaves my insomnia
Traces of stirrups rearing up
and vanishing in columns of smoke
You as well heaps of stones
weary of holding up burial sites
Must I implore you
to bandage the cracks in me
Soles in tatters
on the pathways of convulsion

IX

Et vous bien-aimées
Aux visages
Jalousant le croissant de lune
Ils ont volé vos rires vos airs festifs
Vos bracelets sonores
Je n'ai plus de paumes pour essuyer
Les perles de sueur
Sur le front exsangue
Dites à la caravane d'infortune
Il y a vos désirs pris au dépourvu
Mon émoi empaillé parmi les débris

IX

And you loved ones
your faces
envying the moon's crescent
They've stolen your laughter your festive ways
your clinking bracelets
No palm is left me to wipe
the pearls of sweat
from my paling brow
Tell that caravan of ill-luck
your desires caught there off guard
my feelings straw-stuffed in the debris

X

Il y a vieux désert
Ta transe liée
Aux pieux séniles
Le rythme édifié
Sur mille joues fanées
De mille momies
Le corps factice
Dans la brillance figée
La vérité clouée au pilori

X

There is Old Desert
your trance bound
to the pious and senile
Rhythm put together
on the thousand faded cheeks
of a thousand mummies
Body artificial
in the frozen brilliance
Truth pinned to the pious

XI

Il y a ta mélodie
Au fond de ma gorge
Etouffée par les héritiers repus
Leurs fouets saignant les poètes
Jour et nuit
Dans les recoins des royaumes
Le sang de l'écriture
Remplissant des jarres
Le pilon dans le mortier broyant les vers
Tant de subalternes
Aux aguets des rimes du défi

XI

And there's your melody
 deep in my throat
 stifled by sated inheritors
 Their whips slashing the poets
 Night and day
 in the fissures of the kingdom
 the blood of writings
 filling up jars
 The pestle grinding verses in the mortar
 So many subalterns
 hunting down rhymes of defiance

XII

Il y a vieux désert
Des poètes humiliés
Pour avoir aimé ton nom
Les gardes en face des barreaux
Fauves aux griffes de ciseaux
Héros des arènes de l'infamie
D'autres au verbe comme des tambours
Se prélassent dans les décors
Millionnaires d'un jour
La parole gonflée comme une voile
Ne tarissent de panégyriques sous les dômes

XII

Old Desert there are
poets humiliated
for having loved your name
The guards before their bars
wild beasts with scissor claws
heroes of the arenas of infamy
Others whose words are drums
lounge in various decors
Millionaires that day
their speech swelling like a sail
Panegyrics ever flowing under the domes

XIII

Te revoilà désert
Aux piliers brisés
Dans la litanie des remparts
Les portes ouvertes aux brigands
Il y a le Livre des morts
Remplissant la vallée des Anubis
Il y a les restes âcres de mon acacia
Brûlé au couchant qui décline
Et des échassiers englués
Au dépôt des plumes

XIII

Here you are again Desert
pillars cracking
in the litany of ramparts
Gates open to brigands
There is the Book of The Dead
filling up the valley of Anubis
There are the acrid remains of my thorntree
burned in the fading sunset
and herons trapped
in the storehouse of feathers

XIV

O Selma
Emmurée
A la braise interdite
La taille jetée aux cendres
La hanche éteinte sans étreinte
La sève asséchée
Résine après résine
Cette écorce n'est pas pour parfumer
L'haleine lourde de ton désir
Mais recel de l'embaumeur des momies

XIV

Oh Selma
bricked up
your flame denied
Your waist in the ashes
Hip faded away without embrace
Life saps dried
resin following resin
This husk will perfume
not the heavy breath of your desire
but the mummy embalmer's hoard

XV

Et toi Khawla
A la chevelure offrande pour les séniles
Leurs jambes titubantes
Dans la raideur des tonneaux
Les véhicules ruisselants d'huile
Les cannes branlantes
Et la démesure coquille d'épluchure
De quels sacrifices
Dois-tu satisfaire les colonnes qui s'écroulent
Mer morte sous tant de sel
Rongée par les fers qui se consument

XV

And you Khawla
your hair a lush offering for the senile
Their legs tottering
 under barrel bodies
 Chassis slippery with oil
Trembling canes
 empty shells of their excesses
With what sacrifices
 must you satisfy the crumbling columns
A sea dead under so much salt
 Eaten away by smoldering irons

XVI

Dis désert
Qui abritera de tes tempêtes
La course du faon apeuré
Sans herbe
Tremblant
Parmi les demeures hantées
Désert battu de mille obus
Ce n'est pas une étoile filante
Que tes bras accueillent
Dans la chevauchée des étincelles
Mais mon rêve fossile

XVI

Tell me Desert
who will shelter from your storms
the plunging of the frightened fawn
Grass-starved
trembling
among haunted mansions
Desert battered by endless shrapnel
This is not a shooting star
that your arms enfold
in a galloping of sparks
but my fossil dream

XVII

Dis vieux désert
Qui viendra essuyer ta larme sur la joue
De l'aurore
Les étendards des prétendants
Soulevés de mille armes
Razzias ghazouas continuelles
As-tu châtié les jambières
Dans la chute des guerriers
De défaite en défaite
Leurs sabres vaniteux et inutiles

XVII

Tell me Old Desert
who will come brush the tear
from the cheek of dawn
The banners of the pretenders
raised on a thousand weapons
Razzias and constant religious wars
Have you burnished shin-guards
in the warriors' tumbling
from defeat to defeat
swords useless and vain

XVIII

Et je porte ta pierre
Sur le dos de l'incertitude de l'Histoire
Vieux désert
Les montagnes dévorées par les sauterelles
Vacarmes et mandibules
L'urticaire a envahi mon corps
Blessé par les complaintes cernées de miradors
Le thym est si loin
Séquestré par les murs
Toutes ces sentinelles dans les tours indignes

XVIII

And I bear your stone
on the back of History's uncertainty
Old Desert
The mountains devoured by locusts
mandibles and din
Hives have invaded my body
wounded by laments beneath the watchposts
The thyme is so far away
sequestered by walls
The sentinels set on affronted towers

XIX

O désert enlisé dans les sables mouvants
Dis aux réfugiés sans refuges
Qui emplissent les camps de fortune
Nouveaux voisins de la déchirure
Vous vous multipliez
Sans devenir
Déposés là
Nus
Spoliés
Dépouillés
L'attente jamais écourtée
Les frontières confondues avec les ornières

XIX

Oh Desert mired in your shifting sands
tell the refugees that fail of refuge
that swarm haphazard camps
newfound neighbors of the rift
You multiply us
without becoming
Dumped here
naked
despoiled
denuded
The waiting never relieved
Your frontiers confused with ruts

XX

Et le chagrin
Couvre mon jujubier
Parmi les coloquintes
La fratrie amoindrie par mille tirs
L'arc toujours tendu
La flèche ne ratant jamais sa cible
Dis désert
Où trouver la pluie pour adoucir
Les arbustes aux épines hérissées
Les crinières des casques prises
Pour des branches durcies

X X

And grief
 covers my jujube
 among the bitter apples
 Siblings decimated by a thousand shots
 The bow always drawn
 the arrow always to its mark
 Tell me Desert
 where is the rain to soften
 bushes and thorns bristling
 Plumes of helmets mistaken
 for hardened twigs

XXI

Où trouver désert
Tambours et flûtes
Pour soulever danses et fêtes
Rythmer les palefrois
Libres de rênes
Les scelles enjouées et envolées
Le vent caressant les épis
O grains pleins et vides
Retombés sans nourrir l'utopie
Nulle fourche généreuse
Par-dessus les aires de battage
Mais la paille et les sabots de fer

XXI

Desert where shall we find
drums and flutes
to raise feast and dance
To start the palfrey's rhythm
free from reins
saddles flying lively
The wind caressing sheaves and cobs
O grain both empty and replete
falling without feeding utopias
No generous pitchfork
above the threshing floors
but straw and iron hooves

XXII

Ils asservissent des frères Noirs
Captifs du rêve de survie
Vendus aux marchés de la honte
De quelle ethnie de quelle religion sont-ils
Maîtres de la nausée et de la vilénie
Désert envahi de scorpions
Empoisonné de piqûres
Ecoute la blessure dans ma chair
La soldatesque maîtresse du mauvais sang
Cisaille mes pas saisis de stupeur
Puis-je avancer quand ils reculent

XXII

They enslave Black brothers
captives of the dream of survival
sold at the markets of shame
of what ethnicity of what religion
these masters of nausea and villainy
Desert invaded by scorpions
poisoned by their stings
Listen to the wound in my flesh
the soldierly mistress of bad blood
Shear my footsteps gripped in stupor
May I advance when they step back

XXIII

Et la nuit s'éloigne de la belle étoile
Les roches comme des lamelles coupantes
Ultimi Barbarorum* allumaient les guerres
Les peaux habillées de poils d'hyènes
L'une tombe l'autre se couvre de boue
Ils brûlent des manuscrits jamais lus
Analphabètes de l'imposture
Erigés en oracles les ablutions sans lavoirs
Comment psalmodier ton nom désert
Et prétendre se cuirasser contre les injures

* Spinoza

XXIII

And night pulls away from the sleeper's stars
Rocks like sharp blades
The Ultimi Barbarorum were stokers of wars
skins draped in hyena fur
One falls the next is covered in mud
They're burning manuscripts unread
illiterates of imposture
raised up as oracles ablutions with no bathing place
How to chant your name oh Desert
and claim armor for their insults

XXIV

Je t'aimais
Palmeraie aux portes du silence absolu
Nul nuage dans ton ciel
Mais les cascades roucoulantes
Les colombes apaisées dans la canicule
Les petits ponts
Pour les traversées minuscules
Tous ces ruisseaux offerts
Aux parcelles à l'ombre
Les rouges-gorges en attente du concert
Impatients et habiles

XXIV

I loved you
palm grove with gates unto absolute silence
No cloud in your sky
but cascades of cooing
doves calmed in the heat wave
Tiny bridges
for minuscule crossings
All these rivulets given
to small lots of shade
Robins awaiting the concert
impatient and skilled

XXV

Les écorces des grenades
Remplissaient les tamis
Pour les meilleures teintures
Les couleurs plus légères que nos courses
Par les matins où le soleil s'oublie
De jardin en jardin les talus de palmes
Et l'odeur enivrée de fruits
D'où vous viennent treilles sur le chemin
Tous ces feuillages pour habiller
Ma crainte des rebuffades
Les grappes encore vertes et moi rougi

XXV

Pomegranate rinds
filled the colanders
yielding the finest tints
Colors lighter than our racing
through mornings when the sun forgets itself
From garden to garden the palm slopes
and the drunken scent of fruit
and their trellises on the path
All these leaves to clothe
my fear of being rebuffed
Clusters still green and me turning red

XXVI

Grand-père comme Gandhi
Se nourrissait de peu
Lait de chèvre et semoule rare
Adossé contre le mur d'argile
Près de lui son tapis de prière
Les tresses unies et régulières
La sueur sans jamais tarir
Il remerciait le monde
De ses sept merveilles
Qui se lève le premier
Lui ou le soleil vermeil

XXVI

Grandfather Ghandi-like
scant his nourishment
Goat's milk and grains of semolina
Propped against the clay wall
his prayer rug nearby
Locks tidy and straight
Sweat flowing always
He thanked the world
for its seven wonders
Who rises first
grandfather or the glowing sun

XXVII

Je t'aimais
Oasis bordant la mer de mes dix ans
Tu étais de houle
Et j'étais l'écume légère
Tu étais la sève
Et j'étais la veine du vent
Le rêve bercé par la vague infantile
Le golfe abri contre les écailles des heures
Une saison s'en va
L'autre sonne au seuil de l'âge
Lampe à pétrole
Flamme de tendresse
Couveuse pour longtemps

XXVII

I loved you
oasis by the sea of my ten years
You were a swell
and I was flying foam
You were sap
and I was the vein of the wind
Dream cradled in childhood's wave
Gulf and shelter from the hours' scales shedding
A season drifts away
the next one rings at the doorstep of age
An oil lamp
flame of tenderness
a long time brooding

XXVIII

Palmeraie nourricière
Des pauvres
Accueillant l'oued généreux et avare
Les sources amoureuses des chants
Les bêtes pour la compagnie fidèle
Un dos soutient les jarres
L'autre emporte le flot
Tant de sobriété
Suffisait à la patience
De devancer les sabots
La nudité n'est pas une tare
Mais couvrait le corps si beau

XVIII

Palm grove nourishing
the poor
Welcoming the oued generous or dry
Loving wellsprings of song
Beasts for the loyal gathering
One shoulder bears up the jars
the next bears away the stream
So much sobriety
yielded patience
to set out before the hooves
Nudity is no defect
but covered so lovely a body

XXIX

Et le couchant caressait la plaine
Le bruit des calèches en écho
Les grelots mesurés au galop
Ta fontaine à toi
Etait pleine de rires
L'insouciance reine des leçons
Tes sujets rédigés en envol
Tiraient leurs lignes des trésors
Surpris dans les filets
Oiseaux dans les arbustes
Picorant les fruits à la dérobée
Feinte et simulée jamais obéie

XXIX

And sunset caressed the plain
barouche wheels echoing
harness bells at trotting measure
Your own fountain
brimmed with laughter
Insouciance queen of all lessons
your subjects drafted on the wing
drew their lines from treasures
Caught in nets
the birds of the bush
pecking at fruit in a secrecy
feigned and simulated never obeyed

XXX

Revenant à toi sans cesse
Mais suis-je jamais parti
Les bras chargés de paniers d'osier
Je t'emportais chanson vibrante
L'opulence réduite et tourbeuse
Cela suffisait pour partager l'embellie
Jus de palmier suave pêches et dattes à l'envi
Cette aire pour libérer la poussière
De sa léthargie cours criais-tu à l'animal
L'herbe se mérite l'orge récompense
L'effort et le poids du jour
Sans rechigner aux obstacles
Leurs leurres toujours dressés et renversés

XXX

Coming back to you always
but have I ever left
My arms weighed with wicker baskets
I used to bring you ringing song
opulence condensed and earthy
No more was needed to share the brightening day
coconut water smooth peaches dates always to hand
this acre to free the dust of its lethargy
run you cried to the animal
The grass deserves the reward of barley
The effort and weight of the day
and no halting at obstacles
their fences set and soon knocked down

XXXI

O jardin qui accueilles tabac henné
Champs de trèfles as-tu écouté
Les roseaux au bord des ruisseaux
Le passage des brises par-dessus les rivières
J'étais une liane entre tes verdures
Le guet scellé à l'attente vaine
L'entourage affectueux plus fort
Que la solitude dans la durée
Cette lumière plus riche que la couronne
Des rois reclus dans leurs demeures
Tant de rayons à l'intérieur du cercle
Eclairaient les visages dans la pénombre
Mère souffrante sur son lit
Et toi debout sur le seuil

XXXI

Oh garden welcoming tobacco henna
fields of clover have you listened
to the reeds by the brooks
Breezes passing above the streams
I was a vine in all your green
birdlime set but in vain
The group in its affection stronger
than solitude and more lasting
This light richer than the crown
of kings huddled in their dwellings
Such rays within this circle
Lighting the faces in half-light
A mother suffering on her bed
and you standing at the threshold

XXXII

Désert las de toutes ces batailles
As-tu perdu la palmeraie féconde
Vaincu par les flammes et les fumées
Sous le nuage retenu
D'exil en exil
Le monde vaste et rétréci
Qui dira aux rivages détournés
L'empreinte des distances
Parcourues pour distendre les coques
Carcasses de navires et naufrages voulus

XXXII

Desert weary of all these battles
have you lost your fertile palm grove
Vanquished by flames and smoke
under this cloud held back
From exile to exile
the world vast and shrunken
Who will explain to shorelines deformed
the tracks of the distances
covered to strain these hulls
carcasses of boats and shipwrecks desired

XXXIII

Les tribus jamais rassasiées
De butins de guerre
Leurs haches levées
Contre elles-mêmes
Mausolées qui brûlent
Tombeaux souillés
Elles élevaient le sang
Au rang des mouches
Les cimetières anonymes
La terre pétrifiée
Le mensonge de marbre

XXXIII

Tribes never sated
with the spoils of war
Their axes raised
against themselves
Mausoleums burning
Tombs desecrated
They raised blood up
to the rank of flies
The cemeteries anonymous
The soil petrified
The lie in marble wrought

XXXIV

Où que tu regardes
L'horizon frère de l'incandescence
Le lointain sanglé à l'indécence
De sanctuaire en sanctuaire
Les ténèbres appellent les tirailleurs
La terreur sacrée comme une extase
Dans les tourbillons des derviches tourneurs
L'un chasse l'autre
Illuminé sans paix sublime
Fou de Dieu jusqu'à l'abîme

XXXIV

Wherever you look
horizon a brother to incandescence
distance lashed to indecency
From sanctuary to sanctuary
darkness calls out to the skirmishers
Terror now sacred as an ecstasy
In dust devils whirling dervishes
were chasing each other
shining bright but failing at sublime bliss
God's Crazies unto the abyss

XXXV

J'emportais ton chant
Bercé par le rabâb
Chasseur d'illusions
Parcourant les contrées solennelles
Les peuples sur la cime de l'Olympe
Avisés du sacrifice
Pour confondre les tyrans
Qui leur a appris à marcher
Sur mes songes fraternels
Leurs croyances comme des voyances
De sorcières semaient la discorde
Qui toujours recommence
Les meutes triomphant de la raison

XXXV

I carried away your song
lulled by the rebab
the sweeper of illusions
Spreading through solemn regions
peoples of Olympian peaks
and focused on sacrifice
to confound the tyrants
Who taught them to walk
over my fraternal dreams
Their beliefs sowing discord
like the clairvoyance of sorcerers
and it begins again always
Mobs triumphing over reason

XXXVI

Et la démarche titubante
Courbé par tant de cortèges
Je repoussais tes pliures
Aux repaires des spectres
Ma canne rongée par l'usure
Fallait-il aux félons
Remplir d'ossements
Les niches qu'on achève
Jusqu'au minaret mutilé
Leurs sermons repoussaient
Comme de hideuses verrues

XXXVI

And my gait staggering
bent under corteges
I pushed your swirls off
to the dens of specters
My cane eaten by hard use
Did the treacherous have to
fill with bones
the niches they've created
even in scarred minarets
Their sermons always growing back
like hideous warts

XXXVII

Désert ai-je des cordes pour accompagner
Tes mawwâls
Trouvère à la poursuite du Sud errant
Majnoûn
Aimant et banni aux confins de l'épine
L'épopée
Offensée
Par les tribuns naissants
Leur vaillance en souffrance
Sans relâche pour la relance
De la refonte des césures

XXXVII

Have I the strings Desert to accompany
your mawwâls
wandering minstrel in pursuit of the South
madman
loving and banished to the rows of thorns
The epic
offended
by the new tribunes
their valor in abeyance
No rest in this revival
of revising caesuras

XXXVIII

Désert témoin de tant de crimes
Ils profanent les pays un à un
La terre comme une gibecière
Les faucons avec des œillères
Les cicatrices jamais guéries
Combien de proies faut-il sacrifier
Au champ des victimes
Arabie heureuse de toutes ces élégies
Reliques de l'éclipse reconduite
De siècle en siècle
Les railleurs gardeurs de la relève
Interférant à toute épreuve
Hennissant et immobiles

XXXVIII

Desert witness to so many crimes
They profane the nations one by one
the earth like a game bag
hawks with blinders on
scars never healing
Prey in what numbers sacrificed
in the field of victims
Arabia happy with all these elegies
Relics of an eclipse renewed
from century to century
The scoffers withholding relief
ever interfering
neighing and immobile

XXXIX

Arabie heureuse de tant de bandoulières
La ceinture à la lisière de l'incrédule
Le croissant fertile répondant à tes moussons
As-tu langui de Saba Babylone Palmyre et Syrte
Du Golfe à l'Atlantique
J'entends ton cri
L'appel nourri de fantômes
Au chevet des sarcophages
Ebranlés et affolés dans la froidure
Ce bras pour rassembler les gerbes
Réduit à un manche redevable à l'oubli

XXXIX

Arabia happy with so many shoulder-slings
 belts at the edge of the unbelievers
The fertile crescent responding to your monsoons
Have you pined for Saba Babylon Palmyra & Sirte
From the Gulf to the Atlantic
I hear your cry
An appeal nourished with ghosts
 bedside to sarcophagi
 shaken and crazed in the cold
This arm for gathering the sheaves
 reduced to a handle indebted to forgetting

XL

Désert tu fus vert
De guerre en guerre
Les cavaliers lourds de leurs armures
Perdaient leurs montures
Ni les prophètes n'ont fait jaillir les sources
Ni l'or noir n'a étanché la soif
Face au soleil
Le sphinx est toujours seul
O rosées tempérantes
Apaisez ces vallées
Mais où suspendre les jardins de tournesol
Les terrasses absentes et la floraison difficile

XL

Green you were oh Desert
from war to war
The knights heavy with armor
as they lost their mounts
The prophets summoned up no springs
nor has black gold slaked any thirst
Facing the sun
the Sphinx remains alone
Oh softening dews
appease these valleys
But where to hang the sunflower gardens
terraces absent and blooming repressed

XLI

Charlie Hebdo Le Bataclan Hyper Cascher
Marseille Nice Rouen Djerba Sousse
Le Bardo Tunis Londres Manchester Sidney
Bruxelles Molenbeek Berlin Munich
Ottawa New York Boston Ankara Istanbul
Finlande Saint-Pétersbourg Moscou
Copenhague Madrid Barcelone
Le Caire Le Sinaï La Mecque Irak Syrie
Beyrouth Aden Sanaa Riyad Lybie
Alger Casablanca Kaboul Islamabad
Grand-Bassam Bamako Tombouctou
Mogadiscio Nairobi Nigeria Burkina Faso

O Mou'allaqât!
Comment hisser le poème?
Ils organisent la sauvagerie
Et je n'oublie

Paris, 2015–2018

XLI

Charlie Hebdo the Bataclan Hyper Cacher
Marseille Nice Rouen Djerba Sousse
Bardo Museum Tunis London Manchester Sidney
Brussels Molenbeek Berlin Munich
Ottawa New York Boston Ankara Istanbul
Finland Saint Petersburg Moscow
Copenhagen Madrid Barcelona
Cairo the Sinai Mecca Iraq Syria
Beirut Aden Sanaa Riyadh Libya
Algiers Casablanca Kabul Islamabad
Grand-Bassam Bamako Timbuktu
Mogadishu Nairobi Nigeria Burkina Faso

Oh Mou'allaqât!
How to raise up the poem?
They're organizing savagery
and I won't forget

Paris, 2015–2018

NOTES

IV   In many Arab countries men wait near graves, old & new, to be paid to recite — usually the Koran.

VII   "Incendiaire" refers to suicide vests & other bombing attacks.

XIV   Selma — An archetypal woman's name, and a typical dedication of *Mou'allaqa* poems (see below).

XV   Khawla — A well-known character (woman) in Tarafa ibn Abd al Bakri's *Mouallaqa*. A name often favored by Arab women. ¶ "Raideur des tonneaux" — Bekri has clarified that the poem refers to ponderous old men.

XXIII   Ultimi Barbarorum — Bekri's one footnote cites Spinoza here. The philosopher used the phrase (on a placard, it is said) to protest the murder of the De Witt brothers (1672).

XXIV   The following nostalgic sequence celebrates the "palmeraie," or palm grove — a relatively lush & often extensive area (Bekri grew up in a palmeraie).

XXVIII   "Oued" — A stream or dry stream bed (*wadi* is a variant).

XXX   The final image is of ineffectual fences, meant to contain animals in the grove. This is an example of a nostalgic, and difficult, image on which Bekri offered assistance.

XXXV   "Rebab" — a string instrument, both plucked and bowed.

XXXVII   "Mawwâl" — traditional genre of sung poetry, often the preface to a song.

XLI   "Mou'allaqât" — refers to the seven pre-Islamic odes, poems thought to have been hung on the Kaaba walls in Mecca (see Bekri's preface).

TAHAR BEKRI

The poet was born in 1951 in Gabès, Tunisia.

He has lived in Paris since 1976. Bekri writes in both French and Arabic. His thirty published works comprise poetry, essays, & art books. The poetry, awarded various literary distinctions, has been translated into numerous languages and is studied and commented on in both academic and artistic works. Awards include the French Language and Literature Prize from the Académie Française (2019). Bekri has been Honorary Lecturer at the University of Nanterre.

Most recent publication: *Mon pays, la braise et la brûlure* (Ed. Edern, 2025).

OTHER BOOKS BY TAHAR BEKRI

Published by Al Manar

Les arbres m'apaisent, livre d'art, avec des peintures acryliques
 d'Annick Le Thoër, 2017.

Mûrier triste dans le printemps arabe, 2016.

La nostalgie des rosiers sauvages, peintures d'Annick Le Thoër, 2014.

Poésie de Palestine, anthologie, 2013.

Je te nomme Tunisie, 2011.

Les dits du fleuve, 2009.

Si la musique doit mourir, 2006.

La brûlante rumeur de la mer, 2004.

L'Horizon incendié, 2002.

Published by Elyzad

Le livre du souvenir, 2007; Ed. Poche, 2016.

Au souvenir de Yunus Emre, 2012.

Salam Gaza, 2010.

Published by L'Hexagone

Les songes impatients, 1997; 2ème éd. ASPECT, 2004.

Published by L'Harmattan

Marcher sur l'oubli, conversations avec Olivier Apert, 2000.

De la littérature tunisienne et maghrébine, 1999.

Inconnues Saisons (anthologie personnelle, français-anglais), 1999.

Poèmes à Selma (en arabe), 1996; 1ère éd. Hiwar, Rotterdam, 1989.

Les chapelets d'attache, 1994; 1ère éd. Amiot, 1993.

Littératures de Tunisie et du Maghreb, 1994.

Le Laboureur du soleil, 1991, 1ère éd. Silex, 1983.

Le Cœur rompu aux océans, 1988.

Le Chant du roi errant, 1985.

Published by L'Or du temps

Journal de neige et de feu, (en arabe), 1997.

Published by Artalect

La sève des jours, CD, 2003; cassette, 1991.

ACKNOWLEDGMENTS

The translator is immensely grateful to Tahar Bekri for support in this effort, and for instant response to many queries. And to Alain Gorius, of Editions Al Manar, for generously offering the right to reproduce.

To Rainer J. Hanshe vast *hosanna* for creating what every readership — especially American readership — needs: a translation press.

COLOPHON

THE DESERT AT DUSK
was handset in InDesign CC.

The text & display font is *Albertus*.

Book design & typesetting: Alessandro Segalini

Cover design: CMP

Front cover image: Paul Klee, *Strong Dream* (1929).

Opening image: Petrus Bertius, *Descriptio Regni Tunetani / Carthaginensis sinus* (1603).

THE DESERT AT DUSK
is published by Contra Mundum Press.

Contra Mundum Press   New York · London · Melbourne

CONTRA MUNDUM PRESS

Dedicated to the value & the indispensable importance of the individual voice, to works that test the boundaries of thought & experience.

The primary aim of Contra Mundum is to publish translations of writers who in their use of form and style are *à rebours*, or who deviate significantly from more programmatic & spurious forms of experimentation. Such writing attests to the volatile nature of modernism. Our preference is for works that have not yet been translated into English, are out of print, or are poorly translated, for writers whose thinking & æsthetics are in opposition to timely or mainstream currents of thought, value systems, or moralities. We also reprint obscure and out-of-print works we consider significant but which have been forgotten, neglected, or overshadowed.

There are many works of fundamental significance to *Weltliteratur* (& *Weltkultur*) that still remain in relative oblivion, works that alter and disrupt standard circuits of thought — these warrant being encountered by the world at large. It is our aim to render them more visible.

For the complete list of forthcoming publications, please visit our website. To be added to our mailing list, send your name and email address to: info@contramundum.net

Contra Mundum Press
P.O. Box 1326
New York, NY 10276
USA

2012 *Gilgamesh*
Ghérasim Luca, *Self-Shadowing Prey*
Rainer J. Hanshe, *The Abdication*
Walter Jackson Bate, *Negative Capability*
Miklós Szentkuthy, *Marginalia on Casanova*
Fernando Pessoa, *Philosophical Essays*
2013 Elio Petri, *Writings on Cinema & Life*
Friedrich Nietzsche, *The Greek Music Drama*
Richard Foreman, *Plays with Films*
Louis-Auguste Blanqui, *Eternity by the Stars*
Miklós Szentkuthy, *Towards the One & Only Metaphor*
Josef Winkler, *When the Time Comes*
2014 William Wordsworth, *Fragments*
Josef Winkler, *Natura Morta*
Fernando Pessoa, *The Transformation Book*
Emilio Villa, *The Selected Poetry of Emilio Villa*
Robert Kelly, *A Voice Full of Cities*
Pier Paolo Pasolini, *The Divine Mimesis*
Miklós Szentkuthy, *Prae, Vol. 1*
2015 Federico Fellini, *Making a Film*
Robert Musil, *Thought Flights*
Sándor Tar, *Our Street*
Lorand Gaspar, *Earth Absolute*
Josef Winkler, *The Graveyard of Bitter Oranges*
Ferit Edgü, *Noone*
Jean-Jacques Rousseau, *Narcissus*
Ahmad Shamlu, *Born Upon the Dark Spear*
2016 Jean-Luc Godard, *Phrases*
Otto Dix, *Letters, Vol. 1*
Maura Del Serra, *Ladder of Oaths*
Pierre Senges, *The Major Refutation*
Charles Baudelaire, *My Heart Laid Bare & Other Texts*
2017 Joseph Kessel, *Army of Shadows*
Rainer J. Hanshe & Federico Gori, *Shattering the Muses*
Gérard Depardieu, *Innocent*
Claude Mouchard, *Entangled — Papers! — Notes*

2018 Miklós Szentkuthy, *Black Renaissance*
      Adonis & Pierre Joris, *Conversations in the Pyrenees*
2019 Charles Baudelaire, *Belgium Stripped Bare*
      Robert Musil, *Unions*
      Iceberg Slim, *Night Train to Sugar Hill*
      Marquis de Sade, *Aline & Valcour*
2020 *A City Full of Voices: Essays on the Work of Robert Kelly*
      Rédoine Faïd, *Outlaw*
      Carmelo Bene, *I Appeared to the Madonna*
      Paul Celan, *Microliths They Are, Little Stones*
      Zsuzsa Selyem, *It's Raining in Moscow*
      Bérengère Viennot, *Trumpspeak*
      Robert Musil, *Theater Symptoms*
      Miklós Szentkuthy, *Chapter on Love*
2021 Charles Baudelaire, *Paris Spleen*
      Marguerite Duras, *The Darkroom*
      Andrew Dickos, *Honor Among Thieves*
      Pierre Senges, *Ahab (Sequels)*
      Carmelo Bene, *Our Lady of the Turks*
2022 Fernando Pessoa, *Writings on Art & Poetical Theory*
      Miklós Szentkuthy, *Prae, Vol. 2*
      Blixa Bargeld, *Europe Crosswise: A Litany*
      Pierre Joris, *Always the Many, Never the One*
      Robert Musil, *Literature & Politics*
2023 Pierre Joris, *Interglacial Narrows*
      Gabriele Tinti, *Bleedings — Incipit Tragœdia*
      Évelyne Grossman, *The Creativity of the Crisis*
      Rainer J. Hanshe, *Closing Melodies*
      Kari Hukkila, *One Thousand & One*
2024 Antonin Artaud, *Journey to Mexico*
      Rainer J. Hanshe, *Dionysos Speed*
      Amina Saïd, *Walking the Earth*
      Léon-Paul Fargue, *High Solitude*
      Gabor Schein, *Beyond the Cordons*
      Marquis de Sade, *Stories, Tales, & Fables*
2025 Sara Whym, *Dreamscapes I — Betrayals (101 & 202 Nights)*
      Rainer J. Hanshe, *Humanimality*

SOME FORTHCOMING TITLES

Scott Von, *Autopoesis*
Carmelo Bene, *Lorenzaccio* +

AGRODOLCE SERIES Æ

2020 Dejan Lukić, *The Oyster*
2022 Ugo Tognazzi, *The Injester*

HYPERION
On the Future of Æsthetics   2006–PRESENT

To read samples and order current & back issues of *Hyperion,*
visit contramundumpress.com/hyperion
Edited by Rainer J. Hanshe & Erika Mihálycsa (2014 ~)

CONTRA MUNDUM PRESS

is published by Rainer J. Hanshe
Typography & Design: Alessandro Segalini
Publicity & Marketing: Alexandra Gold
Ebook Design: Carlie R. Houser

·

THE FUTURE OF KULCHUR

From major museums like the MoMA to art house cinemas such as Film Forum, cultural organizations do not sustain themselves from sales alone, but from subscriptions, donations, benefactors, and grants.

Since benefactors of Peggy Guggenheim's stature are rare to come by, and receiving large grants from major funding bodies is an infrequent and unreliable source of capital, we seek to further our venture through a form of modest support that is within everyone's reach.

Although esteemed, Contra Mundum is an independent boutique press with modest profit margins. In not having university, state, or institutional backing, other forms of sustenance are required to move us into the future.

Additionally, in the past decade, the reduction of the purchasing budgets across the nation of both public and private libraries has had a severe impact upon publishers, leading to significant decreases in sales, thereby necessitating the creation of alternative means of subsistence.

Because many of our books are translations, our desire for proper remuneration is a persistent point of concern. Even when translators receive grants for book projects, the amount is often insufficient to compensate for their efforts, and royalties, which trickle in slowly over years, are not a reliable source of compensation.

WHAT WILL BE DONE

With your participation we seek to offer writers and translators greater compensation for their work, and in a more expeditious manner.

Additionally, funds will be used to pay for translation rights, basic operating expenses of the press, and to represent our writers and translators at book fairs.

If the means exist, we will also create a translation residency, providing opportunities to both junior and more established translators, thereby furthering our cultural efforts.

Through a greater collective and the cultural commons of the world, we can band together to create this constellation and together function as a patron for the writers and artists published by CMP. We hope you will join us in this partnership.

Your patronage is an expression of your confidence and belief in visionary literary work that would otherwise be exiled from the Anglophone world. With bookstores and presses around the world struggling to survive, and many even closing, joining the Future of Kulchur allows you to be a part of an active force that forms a continuous & stable foundation which safeguards the longevity of Contra Mundum Press.

Endowed by your support, we can expand our poetics of hospitality by continuing to publish works from many different languages and reflect, welcome, and embrace the riches of other cultures throughout the world. To become a member of any of our Future of Kulchur tiers is to express your support of such cultural work, and to aid us in continuing it. A unified assemblage of individuals can make a modern Mæcenas and deepen access to radical works.

The Oyster ($2/month)

- Three issues (PDFs) of your choice of our art journal, *Hyperion*.
- 15% discount on all purchases (for orders made directly through our site) during the subscription term (one year).
- Impact: $2 a month contributes to the cost to convert a title to an ebook and make it accessible to wider audiences.

Paris Spleen ($5/month)

- Receive $35 worth of books or your choice from our back catalog.
- Three issues (PDFs) of your choice of our art journal, *Hyperion*.
- 18% discount on all purchases (for orders made directly through our site) during the subscription term (one year).
- Impact: $5 a month contributes to the cost purchasing new fonts for expanding the range of our typesetting palette.

Gilgamesh ($10/month)

- Receive $70 worth books of your choice from our back catalog.
- 4 PDF issues of our magazine *Hyperion*.
- A quarterly newsletter with exclusive content such as interviews with authors or translators, excerpts from upcoming titles, publication news, and more.
- 20% discount on all merchandise (for orders made directly through our site) during the subscription term (one year).
- Select images of our books as they are being typeset.
- Impact: $10 a month contributes to the production and publication of *Hyperion*, encouraging critical engagement with art theory *&* æsthetics and ensuring we can pay our contributors.

The Greek Music Drama ($25/month)

- Receive $215 worth of books.
- 5 PDF issues of *Hyperion* ($25 value).
- A quarterly newsletter with exclusive content such as interviews with authors or translators, excerpts from upcoming titles, publication news, and more.
- 25% discount (for orders made directly through our site) on all merchandise during the subscription term (one year).
- Impact: $25 a month contributes to the cost of designing and formatting a book.

Citizen Above Suspicion ($50/month)

- Receive $525 worth of books.
- 6 PDF issues of *Hyperion* ($30 value).
- 1 tote.
- A quarterly newsletter with exclusive content such as interviews with authors or translators, excerpts from upcoming titles, publication news, and more.
- 30% discount on all merchandise (for orders made directly through our site) during the subscription term (one year).
- Select one forthcoming book from our catalog and receive it in advance of release to the general public.
- Impact: $50 a month contributes to editorial & proofreading fees.

Casanova ($100/month)

- Receive $1040 worth of books.
- 7 PDF issues of *Hyperion* ($30 value).
- 1 tote.
- A quarterly newsletter with exclusive content such as interviews with authors or translators, excerpts from upcoming titles, publication news, and more.
- 35% discount on all merchandise (for orders made directly through our site) during the subscription term (one year).
- A signed typeset spread from two forthcoming books.
- Select two forthcoming books from our catalog and receive them in advance of release to the general public.
- Impact: $100 a month contributes to the cost of translating a book, therefore supporting a translator in their craft & bringing a new work & perspective to Anglophone audiences.

Cybernetogamic Vampire ($200/month)

- Receive $2020 worth of books.
- 10 PDF issues of *Hyperion* ($50 value).
- 1 tote.
- A quarterly newsletter with exclusive content such as interviews with authors or translators, excerpts from upcoming titles, publication news, and more.
- 40% discount on all merchandise (for orders made directly through our site) during the subscription term (one year).
- A signed typeset spread from four of our forthcoming books.
- The listing of your name in the colophon to a forthcoming book of your choice.
- Select four forthcoming books from our catalog and receive them in advance of release to the general public.
- Impact: $200 a month contributes to general operating expenses of the press, paying for translation rights, and attending book fairs to represent our writers and translators and reach more readers around the world.

To join the Future of Kulchur, visit here:

contramundumpress.com/support-us